Old-Fashioned Appliqué Quilt Designs

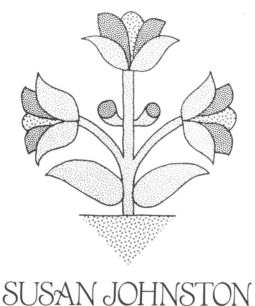

SUSAN JOHNSTON

Dover Publications, Inc.
New York

Publisher's Note

Through these 42 renderings of historic and traditional appliqué quilts, the modern artist and designer can explore a wide variety of usable ideas with an authentic Americana flavor. A number of the designs have rich histories, dating from colonial times. Others are more recent, new variations and embellishments inspired by a vigorous crafts tradition. Many are popular floral motifs, from single flowers, such as Colonial Tulip, to an assortment of flower arrangements and bouquets. A lively, engaging sensibility can be seen at work in these designs that range from the fanciful (Ben Hur's Chariot Wheel) to the homely (Old Town Pump) to the anecdotal (Priscilla Alden). In addition to use in advertising, packaging, illustration and design, these renderings will naturally also be sources of inspiration to quiltmakers. In addition, you might wish to try your hand at coloring some or all of the designs on these pages—either in preparation for a specific project or just for pure enjoyment.

Copyright © 1985 by Dover Publications, Inc.
All rights reserved under Pan American and International Copyright Conventions.

Published in Canada by General Publishing Company, Ltd., 30 Lesmill Road, Don Mills, Toronto, Ontario.

Published in the United Kingdom by Constable and Company, Ltd., 10 Orange Street, London WC2H 7EG.

Old-Fashioned Appliqué Quilt Designs is a new work, first published by Dover Publications, Inc., in 1985.

Design 14 (Cardinal) courtesy Susan McKee's Indiana Heritage Quilt Contest; designs 22 (Poinsettia Basket by Ethel Howey) and 32 (Indiana Wreath) courtesy *Quilter's Newsletter Magazine*; design 25 (Blue Ribbon Bouquet) courtesy *Quiltmaker*.

DOVER *Pictorial Archive* SERIES

Manufactured in the United States of America
Dover Publications, Inc., 31 East 2nd Street, Mineola, N.Y. 11501

Library of Congress Cataloging in Publication Data

Johnston, Susan, 1942–
  Old-fashioned appliqué quilt designs.

  (Dover design library) (Dover pictorial archive series)
  1. Quilting—Patterns. 2. Appliqué. I. Title. II. Series. III. Series: Dover pictorial archive series.
TT835.J64 1985   746.9'7041   84-21103
ISBN 0-486-24845-3 (pbk.)

List of Designs

1. SPRAY OF FLOWERS

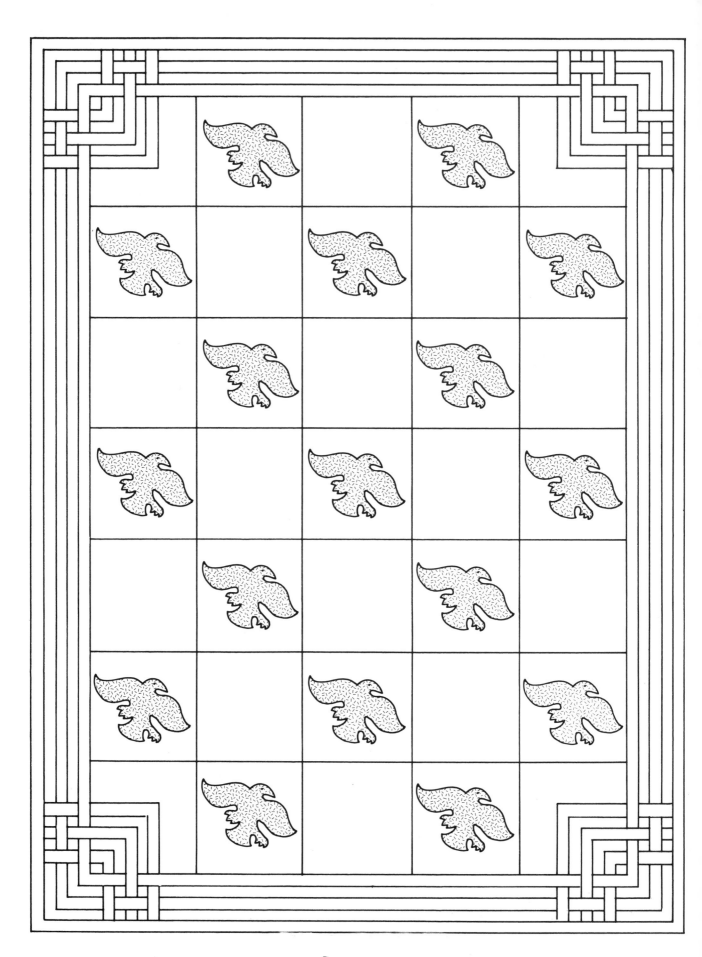

2. EAGLE

3. WHIG ROSE

4. ENGLISH FLOWER GARDEN

5.   OCTOBER FOLIAGE

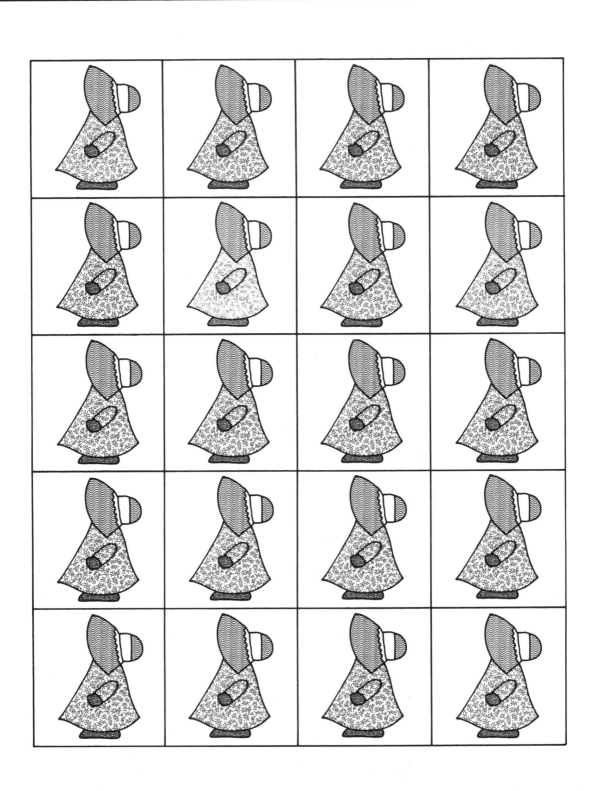

6. SUNBONNET SUE

7. COLONIAL TULIP

8. CONVENTIONAL TULIP

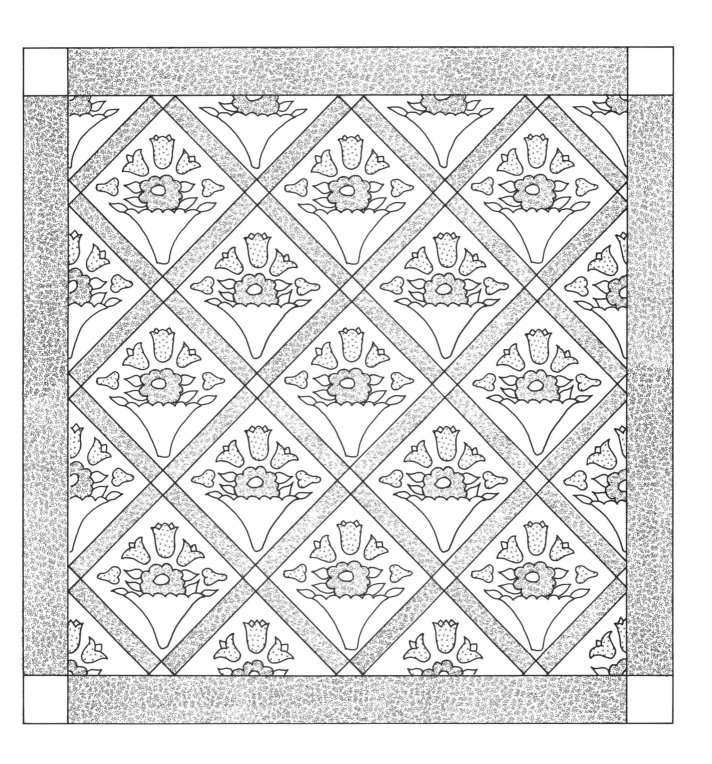

9. NOSEGAY

10. IRIS

11. Design from BALTIMORE BRIDE'S QUILT

12. ROSE

13. MORNING GLORY

14.   CARDINAL

15. ROSE OF SHARON

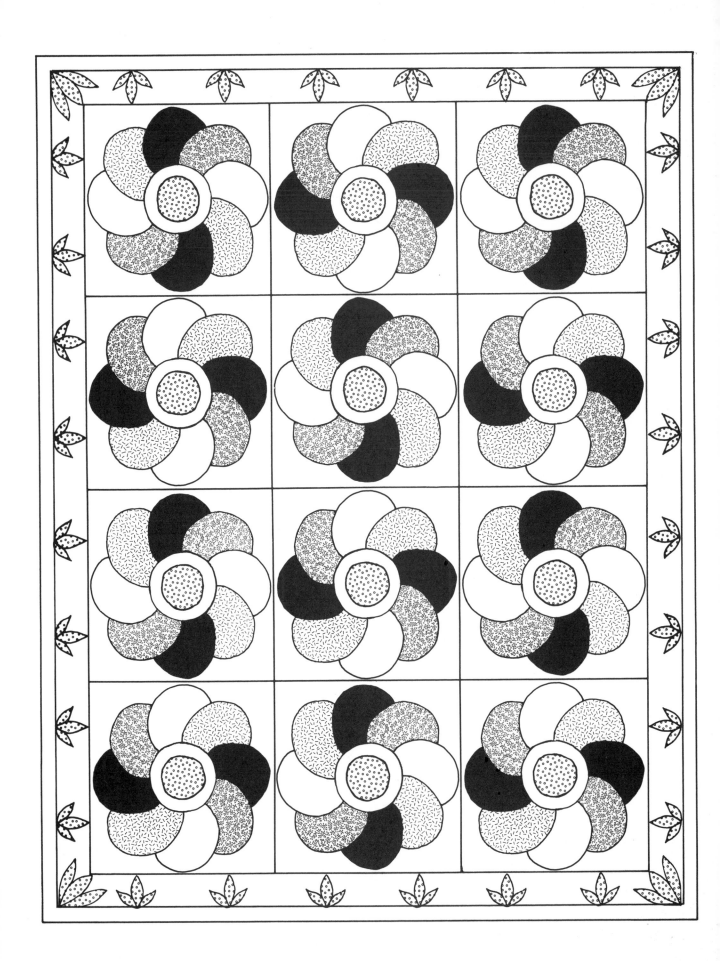

16. PRISCILLA ALDEN

17. BEN HUR'S CHARIOT WHEEL

18. FLOWER BASKET

19. WHIG ROSE

20.   BLUE BLAZES or HONEYBEE

21. WILD ROSE

22. POINSETTIA BASKET

23. PANSY

24. PINEAPPLE

25.   BLUE RIBBON BOUQUET

26. CONVENTIONAL TULIP

27.   WREATH DESIGNS from BALTIMORE BRIDE'S QUILT

28. CHARTER OAK

29. OLIVE'S YELLOW TULIP (corners and center) with TULIP

30. WREATH DESIGN from BALTIMORE BRIDE'S QUILT

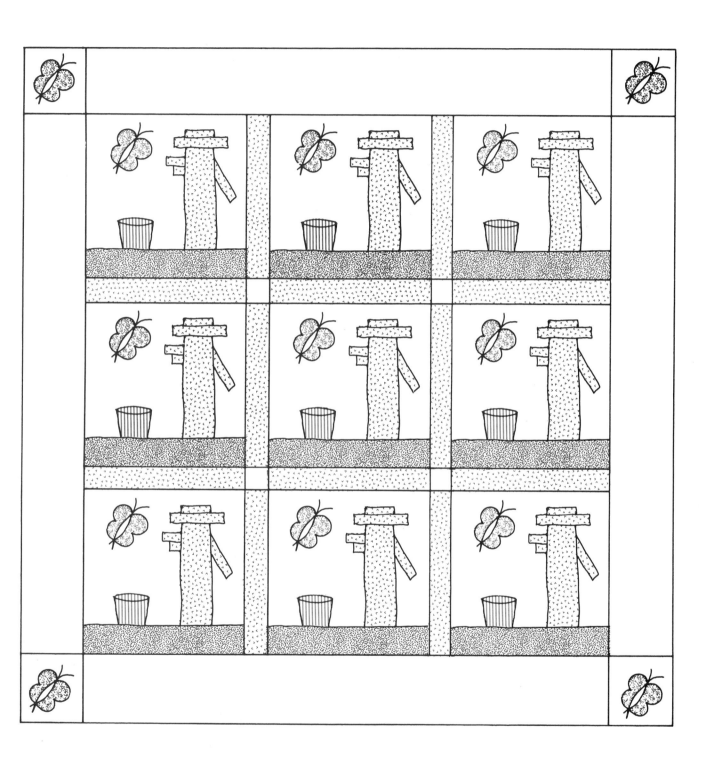

31.　OLD TOWN PUMP

32. INDIANA WREATH set in VARIABLE STAR

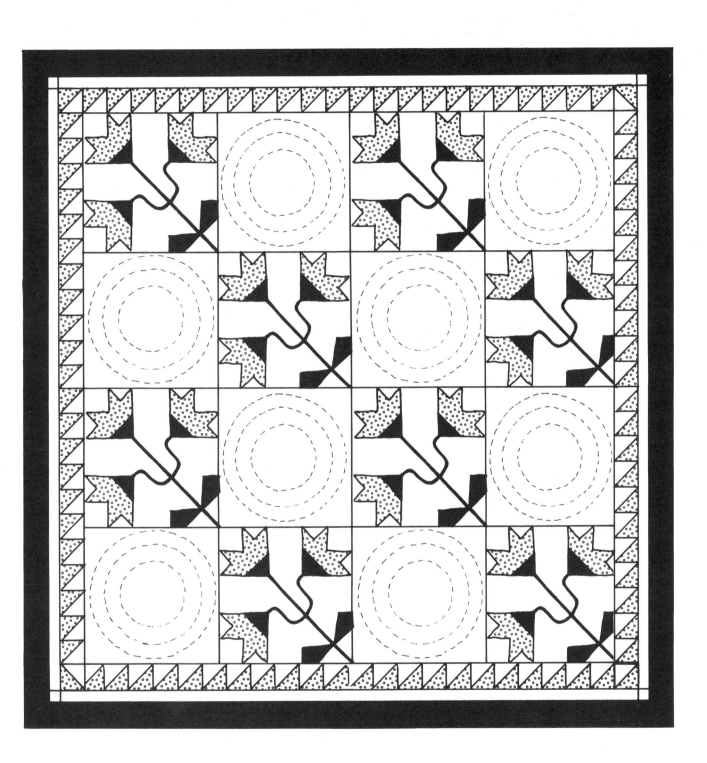

33. DOUBLE TULIP

34.   BALTIMORE BRIDE'S BOUQUET

35. SNOW ON THE MOUNTAIN

36. GRANDMOTHER'S ENGAGEMENT RING or WHIG DEFEAT

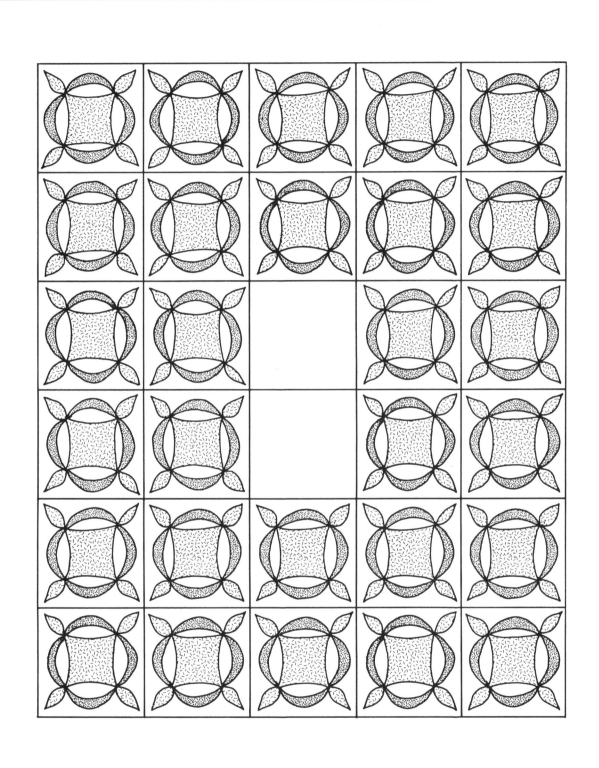

37.   HICKORY LEAF

38. FLOWER ARRANGEMENT

39. TRIPLE TULIP

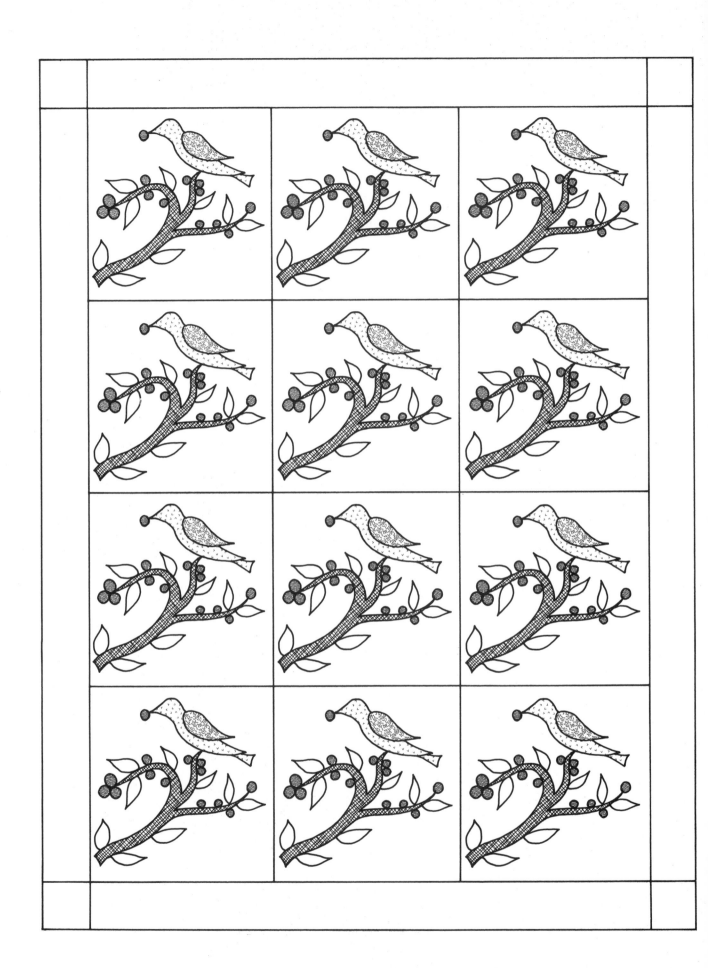

40. THE DOVE

41.   PRESIDENT'S WREATH

42. CUT-PAPER DESIGN